NONFICTION

by Natalie M. Rosinsky

Compass Point Books ✦ Minneapolis, Minnesota

Compass Point Books
151 Good Counsel Drive
P.O. Box 669
Mankato, MN 56002-0669

 This book was manufactured with paper containing
at least 10 percent post-consumer waste.

Managing Editor: Catherine Neitge
Page Production: Bobbie Nuytten
Photo Researcher: Svetlana Zhurkin
Library Consultant: Kathleen Baxter

Art Director: LuAnn Ascheman-Adams
Creative Director: Joe Ewest
Editorial Director: Nick Healy

Compass Point Books would like to acknowledge the contributions of Tish Farrell, who
authored earlier Write Your Own books and whose supporting text is reused in part herein.

Library of Congress Cataloging-in-Publication Data
Rosinsky, Natalie M. (Natalie Myra)
   Write your own nonfiction / by Natalie M. Rosinsky.
      p. cm. — (Write Your Own)
   Includes index.
   ISBN 978-0-7565-4130-9 (library binding)
   ISBN 978-0-7565-4131-6 (paperback)
1. Authorship—Juvenile literature. 2. Reportage literature—Authorship—Juvenile literature. I. Title.
   PN3377.5.R45R67 2009
   808'.042—dc22   2008038465

Visit Compass Point Books on the Internet at *www.compasspointbooks.com*
or e-mail your request to *custserv@compasspointbooks.com*

About the Author
Natalie M. Rosinsky is the award-winning author of more
than 100 works for young readers. She earned graduate
degrees from the University of Wisconsin-Madison and has
been a high school teacher and college professor as well as a
corporate trainer. Natalie, who reads and writes in Mankato,
Minnesota, says, "My love of reading led me to write. I take
pleasure in framing ideas, crafting words, detailing other
lives and places. I am delighted to share these joys with
young authors in the Write Your Own series of books."

Fancy Some Facts

Are you excited by the mysteries that history and science explore? Do you ask yourself "Why?" and "How?" or "What's next?" when you learn about current events? Perhaps you are already a fan of a particular sport or hobby. If you fancy the stories behind facts and you like to investigate them, you will enjoy writing your own nonfiction.

This book will be your guide. It contains brainstorming and training activities to sharpen your writing skills. Tips from famous authors and examples from their work will also help you present intriguing facts and questions with your own personal flair.

CONTENTS

WANT TO BE A WRITER?

This book is the perfect place to start. It aims to give you the tools to write your own nonfiction. Learn how to craft believable portraits of people and interesting storylines with satisfying beginnings, middles, and endings. Examples from famous books appear throughout, with tips and techniques from published authors to help you on your way.

Get the writing habit

Do timed and regular practice. Real writers learn to write even when they don't particularly feel like it.

Create a nonfiction writing zone.

Keep a journal.

Carry a notebook—record interesting events and note how people behave and speak.

Generate ideas

Find an event, discovery, person, or animal whose story you want to tell. What are the problems and accomplishments related to your topic?

Brainstorm to find out everything about your chosen topic.

Research settings, events, and people related to this topic.

Create a timeline of incidents related to the topic.

| GETTING STARTED | SETTING THE SCENE | CHARACTERS | VIEWPOINT |

You can follow your progress by using the bar on the bottom of each page. The orange color tells you how far along the nonfiction writing process you have gotten. As the blocks are filled out, your nonfiction story will be growing.

Plan

What is your nonfiction book about?

What happens?

Plan beginning, middle, and end.

Write a synopsis or create storyboards.

Write

Write the first draft, then put it aside for a while.

Check spelling and dialogue—does it flow?

Remove unnecessary words.

Does the book have a good title and a satisfying ending?

Avoid clichés.

Publish

Write or print the final draft.

Always keep a copy for yourself.

Send your nonfiction work to children's magazines, Internet writing sites, competitions, or school magazines.

| SYNOPSES AND PLOTS | WINNING WORDS | SCINTILLATING SPEECH | HINTS AND TIPS | THE NEXT STEP |

When you get to the end of the bar, your book is ready to go! You are an author! You now need to decide what to do with your book and what your next project should be. Perhaps it will be another nonfiction story, or something completely different.

THE "WRITE" LIFESTYLE

Nonfiction authors may do research in a library, on the Internet, at local museums or government centers, or even in family records and albums. They sometimes travel to interview people and see places connected to the book they are writing.

Just like all writers, nonfiction authors need handy tools and a pleasant, comfortable place for their work. A computer can make writing quicker, but it is not essential.

What you need

These materials will help you organize your ideas and your findings:

- small notebook that you carry everywhere
- paper for writing activities
- large sheet of paper for drawing a timeline
- pencils or pens with several colors of ink
- index cards for recording facts
- files or folders to keep your fact-finding organized and safe
- dictionary, thesaurus, and encyclopedia

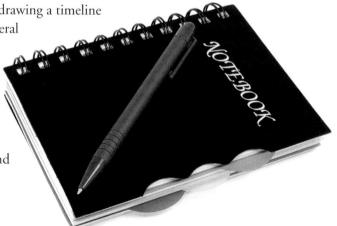

Find your writing place

Think about where you as a writer feel most comfortable and creative. Perhaps a spot in your bedroom works best for you. Possibly a corner in the public library is better. If your writing place is outside your home, store your writing materials in a take-along bag or backpack.

Create a nonfiction writing zone

- Play some of your favorite music or music that is related to your topic.
- Use earplugs if you write best when it is quiet.
- Decorate your space with pictures of your topic's important people, places, or events.
- Place objects that hold good memories from your own life around your space.

Follow the writer's golden rule

Once you have chosen your writing space, go there regularly and often. It is all right to do other kinds of writing there—such as a diary or letters—as long as you *keep on writing!*

Before you can write absorbing nonfiction, you have to build up your writing "muscles." Just as an athlete lifts weights or a musician practices scales, you must train regularly. You cannot wait until you are in the mood or feel inspired.

Tips and techniques
Set a regular amount of time and a schedule for your writing. It could be 10 minutes every morning before breakfast or one hour twice a week after supper. Then stick to your schedule.

Now it's your turn

Family, neighbors, and more

In *Team Moon: How 400,000 People Landed Apollo 11 on the Moon*, Catherine Thimmesh explains how many people contributed to that historic event. Susan Campbell Bartoletti describes how German kids and teens affected world events in *Hitler Youth: Growing Up in Hitler's Shadow*. In *The Great Fire*, Jim Murphy writes about Chicago residents who experienced a terrible disaster in the late 19th century. How have your family, neighbors, or community leaders been part of history?

Brainstorm ideas in your writing place. Take 15 minutes to jot down the stories you have heard at family or neighborhood gatherings. For example, who went to war? Who survived a natural or man-made disaster? Who were immigrants or migrants who moved frequently to find work? Which events, people, or places reappear in the stories you hear? What questions do you still have about these frequently told tales? Do not worry about grammar or spelling as you write—let your ideas and questions flow freely, like water in a rushing stream. You may just have found the inspiration for your own nonfiction book!

Now it's your turn

Fascinating facts

Does a hobby, sport, or particular school subject fascinate you? Perhaps you have close friends or relatives who spend their spare time skiing or painting or playing tennis. Maybe the latest scientific or historical discovery in the news draws your attention. If so, you may already have found just the topic for a personally satisfying nonfiction work.

Tom Owens examines the history of a popular sport in *Football Stadiums.* Cathy Camper combines an interest in insects with research in *Bugs Before Time: Prehistoric Insects and Their Relatives.* Concern for Earth and its creatures inspires Sy Montgomery in *Quest for* the *Tree Kangaroo: An Expedition to the Cloud Forest of New Guinea.* Read one of these books or find two nonfiction books related to your own special interest. See how various authors handle fascinating facts with flair!

CASE STUDY

Award-winning authors Gloria Skurzynski and Susan Campbell Bartoletti (right) both struggled to find time for writing. Skurzynski says, "I wrote nothing longer than grocery lists" until the youngest of her five children started school. Bartoletti was an eighth-grade English teacher for many years. She would get up at 4 A.M. to write before she left for her full-time teaching job.

NOT "JUST THE FACTS, PLEASE"

In the past, nonfiction was often long boooooooring lists of facts. Sad to say, it could be dry as dust.

Author Jim Murphy recalls reading history books that presented "lots of names (usually of famous individuals), lots of dates, and lists of events." They were always very serious and solemn. These qualities frequently made readers dislike nonfiction.

Catherine Thimmesh says that as a kid, "I didn't like it at all." Today Thimmesh writes nonfiction books with the deliberate intention of delighting readers. She says, "Although they are factual, and filled with information, I

want more than anything for kids to be entertained by them." Today's nonfiction writers provide thrills and chills, tears and laughter, along with facts and figures. You can join them as you develop a nonfiction topic that stirs both your heart and mind.

CASE STUDY

Jim Murphy was inspired to write *The Great Fire* by a letter written long ago by 12-year-old Claire Innes. After surviving this destructive blaze in 1881, Claire described her adventure in great detail. Murphy found her letter while researching another book. He said he had no plans to write a book about the Chicago fire, "but I liked Claire's letter enough to copy it down." Years later, Murphy combined Claire's account with other reports by fire survivors in his award-winning book.

Is that a fact?

Sometimes people accept false or incomplete information as facts. Kathleen Krull writes about such mistaken beliefs in *What Really Happened in Roswell? Just the Facts (Plus the Rumors) About UFOs and Aliens* and in *The Night the Martians Landed: Just the Facts (Plus the Rumors) About Invaders from Mars*. Diane Swanson also looks at false "facts" in *Nibbling on Einstein's Brain: The Good, The Bad, & the Bogus in Science*. Read one or more of these books for inspiration.

Now it's your turn

Finding the facts

In your writing place, take 10 minutes to jot down popular sayings. Here are some examples:

- Know the ropes
- Let the cat out of the bag
- As old as the hills
- Blown to smithereens
- Wild goose chase

Where did these phrases come from? If finding out the facts behind a popular saying intrigues you, you may have found the topic for your own nonfiction.

Tips and techniques

Pick a topic based on how interesting —rather than how easy—it seems. Your enthusiasm will ease your way.

FIND YOUR VOICE

Reading many books will help you discover your own style of writing—your writer's voice. Writers continue to develop their voices throughout their lives.

When you read as a writer, you will notice how writers have a rhythm, style, and range of language of their own. Catherine Thimmesh (right) combines many long sentences with a few short ones. Her sentences end powerfully with piles of details. Sy Montgomery's short sentences have a steady, balanced beat. Both Jim Murphy and Kelly Milner Halls use one short sentence to point out a dramatic moment. Halls also uses humor and casual language. Learning to recognize the different techniques writers use to craft their books is like learning to identify different kinds of music.

Writers' voices

Look at the kinds of words and sentences these authors use. Who uses lots of detail? Which writer has a rhythm like a steady drumbeat? Which author uses humor, and which authors are serious? Is there one style you prefer?

We start along an open ridge. The sun beats down, hot. Sweat pours off our faces. Bugs swarm, sip our sweat, suck our blood. But we hardly notice. All that matters is the next step: how to get one foot from here to there.
Sy Montgomery, *Quest for the Tree Kangaroo: An Expedition to the Cloud Forest of New Guinea*

He struggled to get up and, as he did, Sullivan discovered that his wooden leg had gotten stuck between two boards and come off. Instead of panicking, he began hopping toward where he thought the door was. Luck was with him. He had gone a few feet when the O' Learys' calf bumped into him, and Sullivan was able to throw his arm around its neck. Together, man and calf managed to find the door and safety, both frightened, both badly singed.
Jim Murphy, *The Great Fire*

And now, at this defining moment, the world had come together—like nothing ever before—not only to wish the astronauts Godspeed, but to bear personal witness to this incredible event. On that day, people gathered: in homes and schools and businesses; in restaurants and shops; and on sidewalks and streets and in parks. They were eager to be a part, however small, of something so out-of-this-world big. If there was a TV in the vicinity, it was on. And people sat. And watched—wide-eyed, waiting.
Catherine Thimmesh, *Team Moon: How 400,000 People Landed Apollo 11 on the Moon*

Mummies. I saw my first one almost forty years ago as a kid growing up in Friendswood, Texas. When I was about ten years old, my friend sent me a postcard from Mesa Verde National Park in Colorado. "I saw this real live mummy," he had scribbled on the back. But what I saw on the glossy card was definitely dead.
Kelly Milner Halls, *Mysteries of the Mummy Kids*

GET YOUR FACTS STRAIGHT

Avoid mistakes and be thorough. If your topic is family history linked to a major event such as a war or a natural disaster, research what happened then.

Use the library, the Internet, and public records to gather information. Interview other people who shared that experience. If your topic involves science or technology, consult experts such as doctors or engineers for the latest developments.

A timeline will help you avoid errors and keep track of the order of events. Some nonfiction works—such as Cathy Camper's *Bugs Before Time: Prehistoric Insects and Their Relatives*—include such a helpful timeline for readers, too.

Now it's your turn

Time it right!

Draw a long line down the middle of a large sheet of paper. Leave some blank space at the top and bottom. Then make a mark on your timeline for each date important to your topic. Label the dates. To the right of the line write down events connected with the dates. Now do some more research. On the left side of the line, add in other significant events that occurred on the dates—such as wars, natural disasters, or inventions of new technology. Use the blank space at the top and bottom for events that occurred before the timeline began or extended past it. Now you have a timeline connecting your topic to world events.

A good nonfiction book, though, is much more than just a list of dates and facts. Ask questions—in your research or during an interview—that explore people's thoughts and feelings about events.

Now it's your turn

Add the spice of life

To make facts and events come to life, find the answers to such questions as:

- What were your greatest fears or hopes at this time?
- What was the best part of this experience? The worst?
- Who were the most interesting, frightening, or puzzling people or creatures involved in this experience?
- What did you learn from this experience?
- What—if anything—would you do differently today?
- What advice would you give someone who was facing a similar experience?

Tips and techniques

Use a recorder or take notes during an interview to preserve the information you hear. Not everyone is comfortable being recorded, so be certain to ask about this at the beginning of the interview.

CASE STUDY

For her book about the Hitler Youth, Susan Campbell Bartoletti conducted interviews by phone as well as in person. Some people preferred being interviewed in restaurants, while others invited her into their homes. Sometimes Bartoletti found exchanging e-mail messages or letters was the best way to interview a person.

Tips and techniques

Double-check your facts. For his nonfiction, Jim Murphy uses only information that he can confirm in two reliable sources.

BE SENSATIONAL

Help readers experience the settings in your book by describing them in sharp, bright, and clear detail. Draw upon as many senses as you can to re-create each scene.

Jim Murphy helps readers hear, feel, and see what firefighters experienced in blazing Chicago:

> *Two men hauled the cumbersome canvas hose as close to the blaze as possible and aimed a stream of water at the burning building. The water hissed and boiled when it struck the burning wood, sending up a vapor of white steam. The firefighters held their position until the fierce heat began to singe the hair on their heads and arms, and their clothes began to smolder. When the pain became unbearable, they staggered back from the flames for a moment's relief, then lunged forward again.*
> Jim Murphy, *The Great Fire*

We feel as though we are right there, battling alongside these men.

Kathleen Krull paints a vivid picture of New Mexico:

> *The sky goes on forever—electric blue by day, melting into intense reds and purples at sunset, then a forever of blackness at night. Bleached bones dot the white sand below.*
> Kathleen Krull, *What Really Happened in Roswell? Just the Facts (Plus the Rumors) About UFOs and Aliens*

Tips and techniques
Complete the first draft of a book before traveling to its settings. Then you will know what to look for and not miss some of the interesting local connections to your topic.

You may already be familiar with your settings. Or you may be able to travel to visit one of the settings as you are writing about it. Many professional writers try to include travel in their research. For her award-winning book *Secrets of a Civil War Submarine: Solving the Mysteries of the H.L. Hunley*, Sally M. Walker traveled to Charleston, South Carolina, where the *Hunley* sank. Walker says that sitting on the wharf where the crew last docked, she experienced "a sense of connection" to the *Hunley*. She writes that "watching the black porpoises in the harbor, I understood exactly why [people] had called the *Hunley* an 'iron porpoise.'"

CASE STUDY

Sy Montgomery often journeys to distant, dangerous places. She says, "When I find myself swimming with pink dolphins, or face-to-face with a kind of bear no scientist has ever described before, or watching a wild tree kangaroo in a cloud forest, my life feels full enough to contain all the blessings of both adventurer and poet." For several books, Montgomery has planned, traveled, and collaborated with photographer Nic Bishop (with her, right, in New Guinea). She says they work "side-by-side," more closely than "many other writer-photographer collaborators."

GET THE PICTURE

Photographs, paintings, or videos of a setting can inspire you as you write. These aids are especially important if your topic is set long ago or far away. You may not be able to journey through time or visit a distant land, but your imagination can take you and your readers anywhere!

Jim Murphy describes a busy Philadelphia street as it was in 1793:

> *Here three city blocks were crowded with vendors calling their wares while eager shoppers studied merchandise or haggled over weights and prices. Horse-drawn wagons clattered up and down the cobblestone street, bringing in more fresh vegetables, squawking chickens, and squealing pigs. People commented on the stench from Ball's Wharf, but the market's own ripe blend of odors—of roasting meats, strong cheeses, days-old sheep and cow guts, dried blood, and horse manure—tended to overwhelm all others.*
> Jim Murphy, *An American Plague: The True and Terrifying Story of the Yellow Fever Epidemic of 1793*

This detailed description helps readers understand the city where an illness suddenly strikes and spreads.

Now it's your turn

Live in the moment

Carefully look at a video clip, a photograph, or a painting of your setting. Notice all the details. Now write a 100-word description of that place as though you were right there. What do you see or smell? How hot or cold is it? What else do you feel as you brush up against objects or people in this setting? Who else is there? What do the expressions on their faces suggest that they are feeling? What noises or conversations do you hear?

CASE STUDY

Kelly Milner Halls takes readers around the globe with her stories about mummies, including mummified children. *Mysteries of the Mummy Kids* is illustrated with photographs from museums in Chile, Great Britain, and the Netherlands. The University of Alaska and the U.S. Library of Congress—along with mummy hunters—also provided photos.

Follow the map

Books sometimes include maps to help readers understand the geographical relationships and events described in their pages. *Mysteries of the Mummy Kids* has maps of ancient lands where mummies have been found. In *Tracking Trash: Flotsam, Jetsam, and the Science of Ocean Motion*, maps show ocean currents rather than the typical land routes. How scientists investigate these currents fascinated author Loree Griffin Burns so much that she wrote a book.

Tips and techniques

Many museums and government agencies have Web sites displaying their collections of photographs, paintings, and maps. Use these great resources for your setting.

Tips and techniques

Not a photographer your-self? Ask a friend or relative for help. Suzanne Jurmain's brother David Tripp took many of the photos for her book The Forbidden Schoolhouse: The True and Dramatic Story of Prudence Crandall and Her Students, *including a photo of the house itself.*

DISCOVER YOUR HERO

Whether you chose to write about a well-known hero, an ordinary person in extraordinary times, or even a villain, you now have the job of making readers know and care about this person.

To have this connection, readers need to understand what your main character thought and felt at various points in his or her life.

Build a picture

If your subject lived long ago or far away, you may need to give readers information about that time and place. In *Mysteries of the Mummy Kids*, Kelly Milner Halls writes about ancient civilizations such as the Incan empire. She explains how some "children of the Incan empire were sacrificed to ancient gods to ward off bad weather or natural disasters, to improve the health of the Emperor, or to better the Incas' odds in war." Such information helps readers understand why and how these sacrificed kids became mummies. Details bring us onto the scene of a discovery in Chile:

> *Wrapped in a colorful, woven blanket, his arms adorned with copper bracelets, his hair neatly braided in more than two hundred rows, the Incan boy was between seven and nine years old when he closed his eyes for the last time.*
> Kelly Milner Halls, *Mysteries of the Mummy Kids*

The items buried with this boy and his careful grooming show that he was respected.

In *The Forbidden Schoolhouse: The True and Dramatic Story of Prudence Crandall and Her Students,* Suzanne Jurmain gives background details about the "great national battle over slavery" that had begun in 1831 just as Prudence Crandall opened her school for black girls and young women. This information helps readers understand how unusual and brave Crandall was.

Heroic qualities

Does your subject display bravery in actions or words? What other heroic qualities does this person have? In *The Great Fire*, 12-year-old Claire Innes was physically brave, loyal, and loving. She wrote in her letter, "My legs and arms and back [were] all burnt where my dress caught fire." Claire put out that fire, though, and struggled through the crowded streets. She said, "I had to find my family in all of this."

Prudence Crandall was brave in a different way. She fought against the beliefs of townspeople and risked her income as a schoolteacher when she opened her school to a black student named Sarah Harris. Crandall declared, "The school may sink, but I will not give up Sarah Harris." As an adult, Sarah Harris Fayerweather (left) was a strong abolitionist and named her daughter after Prudence Crandall.

HEROES AREN'T PERFECT

Even heroes have flaws and problems. Displaying these weaknesses presents an accurate and sometimes more sympathetic picture for readers.

During the yellow fever epidemic of 1793, Dr. Benjamin Rush (right) worked endlessly to save lives. Yet Jim Murphy notes in *An American Plague: The True and Terrifying Story of the Yellow Fever Epidemic of 1793* that Rush was so proud and stubborn that he took any "challenge … as a personal attack." He would not consider ways of treatment other than his own.

Kelly Milner Halls explains that unlike the honored children sacrificed by the Incas, kid mummies in northwestern Europe were often children with physical problems. They were slain because their own people despised such weakness. The mummy of one 7-year-old boy discovered in Germany demonstrated that. This crippled boy had struggled while being slain. He did not receive a drink to lull him into a peaceful death, the way honored Incan children did. These details help readers sympathize with this boy.

Tips and techniques

Libraries and government archives often keep the letters of famous people and may make these papers available online. Collections of such letters are sometimes also published in books. Local historical societies may have records, journals, memorabilia, and letters of community leaders and some of your ancestors. Family members may have saved letters, documents, and other items from past generations, too.

Build character

Help readers really see your hero or heroes. Use your own vivid words. Add the eloquent descriptions of others. Sy Montgomery uses scientist Lisa Dabek's impressions as well as her own to describe the rare tree kangaroo:

> *"It looked like a big stuffed animal!" she [Dr. Dabek] remembers. Or something that Dr. Seuss might have dreamed up. Impossibly soft, with a rounded face, button eyes, pink nose, pert upright ears and a long thick tail. It was about the size of a small dog or an overweight cat, with plush brown and golden fur.*
> Sy Montgomery, *Quest for the Tree Kangaroo: An Expedition to the Cloud Forest of New Guinea*

Tips and techniques

Journals, diaries, or letters are good sources for physical descriptions of characters as well as events. In Quest for the Tree Kangaroo: An Expedition to the Cloud Forest of New Guinea, *Sy Montgomery kept a written journal of her experiences. Published autobiographies or biographies of well-known people important to your topic are also great sources of information.*

CASE STUDY

"A dramatic situation is nice," Jim Murphy remarks, "but history really comes alive when I can use the first-hand accounts—excerpts from letters, memoirs, journals, diaries, and recollections—of people who were actually there."

Your hero may face problems caused by other people. Or your subject's difficulties may be the result of larger situations beyond anyone's control—war, illness, or natural disasters. Identify the different sources of your subject's problems and bring these to life for the reader.

What is the motive?

People commit evil deeds for different reasons. If there are human villains in your book, are they motivated by greed? By fear? By the desire for power? Or do they believe that their acts are not really evil at all? If people or wild creatures kill animals for food, to what extent are these hunters evil?

Villainous acts

Youths and soldiers brutally carry out government teachings and laws:

Foreign newspapers relayed stories of "Jew hunts," where Hitler Youth and Storm Troopers plunged into nightclubs, theaters, and cafes, dragging out every customer who looked like a Jew and beating him bloody on the sidewalk. As the Hitler Youth marched through neighborhoods, they sang hateful songs with lyrics such as, "When Jew blood spurts from the carving knife / Oh, it's that much more okay!"
Susan Campbell Bartoletti, *Hitler Youth: Growing Up in Hitler's Shadow*

Hunters kill a wild creature until few of its kind remain:

> To most tree kangaroos, people are frightening enemies. With bow and arrow, sometimes with the help of dogs, people have hunted and eaten them for hundreds of years.
> Sy Montgomery, *Quest for the Tree Kangaroo: An Expedition to the Cloud Forest of New Guinea*

Develop a supporting cast

Add details or descriptions that bring minor characters in your book to life. Just a sentence or two or even a few words can make an enormous difference. Sally M. Walker describes a scientist with a vivid comparison:

> *Scott Harris, the* Hunley *team's geologist, is an expert in this highly specialized field. He reads sediment layers like other people read the pages of a book.*
> Sally M. Walker, *Secrets of a Civil War Submarine: Solving the Mysteries of the H.L. Hunley*

Kelly Milner Halls uses dialogue and description to show the reaction by Claus Andreasen, the curator at the Greenland National Museum in Nuuk, to newly discovered mummies:

> *Andreasen was also moved when he saw the infant, whose tiny eyelashes were still intact. But it was one of the adult women who took his breath away. "One of the mummies that looked pregnant was lying with her hands on her stomach, in the way a pregnant woman would sit," he said. Of course, experts try to remain professional, but Andreasen and his team were only human. Overwhelmed by what they found, they had to take a break before they could finish preparing the mummies for transport.*
> Kelly Milner Halls, *Mysteries of the Mummy Kids*

Well-written minor characters will add depth to your nonfiction.

CHOOSE A POINT OF VIEW

Who will tell the story or stories in your nonfiction book— someone who knows everything that happened and what everyone in it thought and felt?

Perhaps you believe your hero would be the best person to tell at least some of the book's events. You might decide that these events should be told from the viewpoints of several of the people who experienced them. Before you write this work, you must choose a point of view for it.

Omniscient viewpoint

Nonfiction works are often told at least in part from the all-seeing and all-knowing—the omniscient—point of view. This permits the writer to include explanations of settings and events that readers might not know. For instance, Jim Murphy informs readers that "Fires were common in all cities back then, and Chicago was no exception." He then lists several Chicago blazes that occurred before the Great Fire of 1881. The omniscient viewpoint also permits a writer to explain any gaps in our knowledge about events that occurred long ago.

Describing an ancient mummy, Kelly Milner Halls writes about his death:

> [T]he seven-year-old Kayhausen Boy may have been singled out by leaders in his community because of his physical disability. But because so little is known about this child—no written records were kept or preserved—we can't be sure. We can only guess, based on what little physical evidence we have.
> Kelly Milner Halls, *Mysteries of the Mummy Kids*

Tips and techniques
Use phrases such as "Some say that" and "As far as we know" to introduce information that cannot be proven true.

First-person viewpoint

The omniscient viewpoint is often effectively combined with other points of view. The first-person viewpoint, using "I" or "we," permits readers to hear someone's inner thoughts or actual speech. Sy Montgomery (right) often writes from the first-person viewpoint as she describes the New Guinea expedition:

> *I'm Sy Montgomery, forty-seven. I wrote the words in this book. ... All of us prepared for the trip carefully. We all got shots to prevent tropical diseases. We brought pills to protect us from malaria. We stuffed our backpacks with rain gear and fleece jackets, water bottles and bug repellent.*
> Sy Montgomery, *Quest for the Tree Kangaroo: An Expedition to the Cloud Forest of New Guinea*

Responsible writers of nonfiction use first-person viewpoint only for words that people actually spoke or wrote, according to records. After double-checking their accuracy, writers place quotation marks around these words or sentences. Montgomery does this as she quotes one of her companions, who jokes about their rain-soaked adventure:

> *"Look—I'm SpongeBob Wetpants!" Toby could be speaking for all of us. In the morning, everything is soaked. We pull on wet socks, wet pants, wet shoes.*
> Sy Montgomery, *Quest for the Tree Kangaroo: An Expedition to the Cloud Forest of New Guinea*

For a full picture of events, nonfiction authors often combine the first-person viewpoint with others, such as an omniscient or third-person viewpoint.

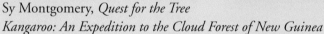

THIRD-PERSON VIEWPOINT

The third-person viewpoint follows the experiences, thoughts, and feelings of one character, who only knows what other characters think or feel by observing or interacting with them. The author refers to this narrator by the person's name and "he" or "she."

Suzanne Jurmain uses third-person viewpoint, combined with first-person viewpoint, to tell much of teacher Prudence Crandall's story:

Opening the school had been a hundred times harder than Prudence had imagined. Of course, she'd known that some people would object to black students. ... Nothing had prepared her for this "present state of adversity." But she'd made up her mind. She wasn't going to give up. "I trust God will help me keep this resolution," she wrote.
Suzanne Jurmain, *The Forbidden Schoolhouse: The True and Dramatic Story of Prudence Crandall and Her Students*

PRUDENCE CRANDALL,
PRINCIPAL OF THE CANTERBURY, (CONN.) FEMALE
BOARDING SCHOOL.

RETURNS her most sincere thanks to those who have patronized her School, and would give information that on the first Monday of April next, her School will be opened for the reception of young Ladies and little Misses of color. The branches taught are as follows:—Reading, Writing, Arithmetic, English Grammar, Geography, History, Natural and Moral Philosophy, Chemistry, Astronomy, Drawing and Painting, Music on the Piano, together with the French language.

☞The terms, including board, washing, and tuition, are $25 per quarter, one half paid in advance.

☞Books and Stationary will be furnished on the most reasonable terms.

For information respecting the School, reference may be made to the following gentlemen, viz.—

ARTHUR TAPPAN, Esq. ⎫
Rev. PETER WILLIAMS,
Rev. THEODORE RAYMOND
Rev. THEODORE WRIGHT, ⎬ N. YORK CITY.
Rev. SAMUEL C. CORNISH,
Rev. GEORGE BOURNE,
Rev. Mr HAYBORN, ⎭

Mr JAMES FORTEN, ⎫ PHILADELPHIA.
Mr JOSEPH CASSEY, ⎭

Rev. S. J. MAY,—BROOKLYN, CT.
Rev. Mr BEMAN,—MIDDLETOWN, CT.
Rev. S. S. JOCELYN,—NEW-HAVEN, CT.
Wm. LLOYD GARRISON ⎫ BOSTON, MASS.
ARNOLD BUFFUM, ⎭
GEORGE BENSON,—PROVIDENCE, R. I.
Canterbury, Ct. Feb. 25, 1833.

Multiple third-person viewpoint

Using multiple points of view adds drama to a nonfiction book. In *The Great Fire*, Jim Murphy details the experiences of seven other people besides Claire Innes. Murphy even explains his choice of multiple viewpoints in this book's introduction. He writes, "Through the eyes of all these people you will see the fire from many distinct vantage points, and feel a wide range of emotions as the hot breath of the fire draws nearer and nearer."

In *Hitler Youth: Growing Up in Hitler's Shadow*, Susan Campbell Bartoletti also combines multiple third-person viewpoints with her omniscient overview. She organizes each chapter around the experiences of particular young people. Most joined and supported this Nazi youth movement, but a few questioned and rebelled against it. Bartoletti also interviewed several Jews who as young people suffered at the hands of classmates.

Now it's your turn

Seeing other points of view

Experiment with your choice of viewpoints. Think about a significant event in your book. Take 10 minutes to write a paragraph about this event from a third-person viewpoint. Then write another paragraph telling this story from the viewpoint of a different person or creature involved in it. Which completed paragraph is more interesting to read? Do you have any researched first-person words you can add to this paragraph? Include these or substitute them for some of your own. How does the addition of a first-person voice make your paragraph more or less interesting?

CHAPTER 5: SYNOPSES AND PLOTS

TELL THE STORY'S STORY

As your nonfiction work takes shape in your mind, it is a good idea to describe it in a paragraph or two. This is called a synopsis.

If someone asked, "What is your book about?" these paragraphs would be the answer. An editor often wants to see a synopsis of a book before accepting it for publication.

Study back cover blurbs

Studying the information on the back cover of a book—called the blurb—will help you write an effective synopsis. A good blurb contains a brief summary of a book's content. It also gives the tone of the book—whether it is serious or funny. Most important of all, the blurb makes readers want to open the book and read it cover to cover! That is certainly true of this tempting blurb from Kelly Milner Halls' *Mysteries of the Mummy Kids*:

Mummies enfold mysteries that may be thousands of years old. For example, did you know that ...
> *... not all mummies are wrapped with cloth?*
> *... not all mummies are found in Egypt?*
> *... some mummies have been on display for centuries?*
> *... some mummies were frozen for centuries?*
> *... some people became mummies by accident?*

And some mummies are thousands of years old—but are still children.
Look inside to unwrap the ... MYSTERIES OF THE MUMMY KIDS.

Make a story map

One way to plan your book is to think of it the way filmmakers prepare a movie. They must know the main story episodes before the cameras start shooting. You can do this for your nonfiction book. The blurb and timeline you wrote will help you here.

Now it's your turn

Lights! Camera! Action!

Write a blurb for the book you plan to write. Summarizing it in one or two paragraphs will sharpen your ideas about your topic. This blurb will help you understand which parts you want to emphasize.

Reread your blurb. Use it to identify the most important events on the timeline of your topic. You are now ready to sketch the "scenes" for the book's story. This is what filmmakers do when they plan the sequence of events in a movie. Under each sketched scene, jot down brief notes about what you will mention about this event. Use this series of sketches, which filmmakers call a storyboard, as a helpful outline as you write the book. If your work has chapters, each scene may be a separate chapter. Perhaps two or more scenes will fit together well in one chapter.

Write a chapter synopsis

Another way to plan your book is to write a chapter synopsis. Look at the timeline again. Group major events there into six to 10 categories, such as plans, setbacks, and successes. Use each of these categories as a chapter. Following a chapter synopsis as an outline is one helpful way to keep on track as you write.

BAIT THE HOOK

Now that you have planned your book, how will you catch and keep the reader's attention? You might choose fascinating first sentences to reel readers into your work.

The sentences could place readers immediately on the scene:

> *It feels like we've walked into a living fairy tale. Our heads are literally in the clouds. Though we're just a few degrees south of the Equator, we're bathed in cool mist. We're 10,000 feet up in the mountains.*
> Sy Montgomery, *Quest for the Tree Kangaroo: An Expedition to the Cloud Forest of New Guinea*

The sentences could establish a comfortable, personal connection with the reader:

> *As a brand-new baby, you couldn't tell day from night. You cried whenever you were hungry.*
> *By the time you were two years old, you mostly slept through the dark hours and stayed awake during the daylight hours.*
> Gloria Skurzynski, *On Time: From Seasons to Split Seconds*

The sentences could be intriguingly mysterious:

> *Something stunning happened in Roswell, New Mexico, in 1947. This unique incident had to do with aliens. Many stories have been told about it.* Kathleen Krull, *What Really Happened in Roswell? Just the Facts (Plus the Rumors) About UFOs and Aliens*

The sentences could shock readers with a bold statement:

> *Science fiction stories and movies predict that insects will take over the world someday. But scientists who work with insects know that bugs have already taken over! There are more species of insects on earth than there are of any other living thing—nearly one million different kinds of insects that we know about, and **millions more that we haven't discovered.*** Cathy Camper, *Bugs Before Time: Prehistoric Insects and Their Relatives*

The style of the opening sentences should fit your topic and the voice you use throughout the book.

HOOK YOUR READERS

You might decide to hook readers with an entire chapter filled with excitement and drama.

That is how Catherine Thimmesh begins *Team Moon: How 400,000 People Landed Apollo 11 on the Moon*. She does not start her book with the years of preparation needed for this achievement. Instead, Thimmesh opens with people around the globe watching the historic moon landing on their TVs. Once she has readers hooked by this excitement, Thimmesh goes back in time to present information. Only then does she begin to tell the story of *Apollo 11* in chronological order.

CASE STUDY

Catherine Thimmesh's dedication in *Team Moon: How 400,000 People Landed Apollo 11 on the Moon* is eloquent. She begins, "For the kids of all those thousands and thousands of people who worked on *Apollo*. For the sacrifices you made—the birthday parties, ballgames, and bedtime stories that your parents had to miss because the moon was calling, and demanding their time. It must have been hard sometimes. But look at what they did! Thanks for sharing them with the world when we needed them most."

Tips and techniques
Some nonfiction books begin with a separate dedication page—a few words, paragraphs, or even a full page in which authors thank people who have helped or inspired them as they wrote the book.

Now it's your turn

Lively beginnings

In the library or a bookstore, look at the opening chapters of various nonfiction books. See which techniques they use to hook readers. How many begin with an exciting event that is taken out of its chronological order? Which methods of beginning a book do you enjoy reading? Which method do you think you will use? Brainstorm sentences and think of dramatic events you could use to begin the book you are planning. Write out several openings to discover the one you find most satisfying.

Loree Griffin Burns uses a fascinating historical figure to hook readers into her book about modern-day science and events. She writes:

Benjamin Franklin, the famous inventor and patriot, was one of America's earliest ocean scientists. Although he eventually conducted experiments at sea, Franklin's early interest in the ocean stemmed from his job as deputy postmaster general of the American colonies. Loree Griffin Burns, *Tracking Trash: Flotsam, Jetsam, and the Science of Ocean Motion*

The author then explains how Franklin (right) talked to ships' captains who carried mail across the Atlantic Ocean. From them, he learned about ocean currents. Burns continues to develop this story of ocean science in chronological order. She summarizes events until the 1990s, when several shipping accidents sparked her own interest in ocean trash. Burns gives events from then onward the most time and space in her book.

BUILD THE SUSPENSE

After your exciting opening, do not let the excitement die! Keep and build suspense for your readers by crafting the book in ways that emphasize the drama in events and situations.

Thrills and chills

Keep your readers on the edge of their seats by hinting about unusual, unexpected, or unpleasant events that will occur in the future. This writing technique—called foreshadowing—will have readers eagerly turning pages to find out what happens next. Jim Murphy uses foreshadowing when he ends a chapter with this thrilling sentence:

> *What followed was a series of fatal errors that set the fire free and doomed the city to a fiery death.*
> Jim Murphy, *The Great Fire*

The suspense is dreadful as we move swiftly from this cliffhanger to the next chapter to see how this tragedy unfolds.

Another way of creating suspense is to show how little characters know or understand compared to readers of the book. This technique—called dramatic irony—is used throughout *The Great Fire*. Readers know the blaze's terrible effects, but Murphy's chronological account shows that victims at first did not realize the danger. Claire Innes was asleep when the alarms sounded. She wrote, "I turned over and closed my eyes again." Horace White, a *Chicago Tribune* editor, reported, "I did not deem it worthwhile to get up and look at it [the fire], or even to … learn where it was." Readers wait to see how and when these people discovered their terrible danger.

Sometimes authors use the present tense to make their chronological accounts of events more suspenseful:

> *And that's where we're standing now. We're hoping we can capture this beautiful tree kangaroo, just for a short time. We hope to outfit it with a radio collar. By following the radio signal ... we want to track the animal through the dense forest—even when we can't see it. This way we can learn and we can help.*
> Sy Montgomery, *Quest for the Tree Kangaroo: An Expedition to the Cloud Forest of New Guinea*

Readers wait and hope along with the expedition members. We experience *their* suspense.

Tips and techniques

Have an unusual topic or approach to a subject? If so, write an opening author's note —a preface or foreword—for your book. This extra introduction contains background material that readers may not know. Susan Campbell Bartoletti's foreword in Hitler Youth: Growing Up in Hitler's Shadow *explains her approach:* "This is not a book about Adolf Hitler. ... Hitler counted on Germany's boys and girls. This is their story."

MYSTERIES TO SOLVE

When there are mysteries to solve, other ways of organizing information besides chronology can be useful. Cause and effect is one important method.

Tips and techniques
Consider several possible ways of organizing your information:
- *Chronology*
- *Cause and effect*
- *Compare and contrast*
Using more than one method may work best for you.

Kathleen Krull uses several methods of organization to explore a mystery. What did people in 1947 *really* see in Roswell, New Mexico? Within her chronological account of events, Krull examines several possible causes of the effects witnesses described. She compares and contrasts how reliable these possibilities are. Similarly, Sally M. Walker explains how scientists, over a period of time, look at human error and equipment failure as possible causes of a submarine's sinking.

By explaining how ice and bogs as well as dry heat create mummies, Kelly Milner Halls is able to discuss kid mummies found around the globe. She then compares and contrasts the views various communities had about these children.

Tips and techniques

Some interesting or important information may not fit smoothly into your book's sequence of events. Put these nuggets of information into sidebars.

CASE STUDY

In *Tracking Trash: Flotsam, Jetsam, and the Science of Ocean Motion*, sidebars provide background information about Earth and its oceans. The geographic coordinates of longitude and latitude, the scientific terms for waves, and the tiny sea creatures called plankton are all explained in sidebars.

Now it's your turn

What's *that* about?

Use logic to group the events in your book into six to 10 chapters. Have fun thinking of a title for each chapter that explains or strongly suggests its content. Choose chapter titles that capture the reader's attention. Jim Murphy's *The Great Fire* includes chapters titled "A Surging Ocean of Flame" and "The Ghost of Chicago."

END WITH A BANG

Conclude your nonfiction book by spotlighting its most dramatic moment.

Like fictional tales, nonfiction builds suspense until it reaches a climax. After this dramatic point, the characters' main problems are over or mysterious questions are answered. Sometimes these conclusions are happy, but sometimes the results are sad, disturbing, or incomplete.

The climax

Suzanne Jurmain describes how Prudence Crandall was jailed, went to court, and survived a fire that was mysteriously set at her school for black girls. Crandall did not give up. After all these events, however, a violent nighttime attack on the school was more than Prudence could stand:

The residents were fast asleep when a bloodcurdling shriek ripped through the darkness. Screaming men pounded the school doors, walls, and windows with clubs and iron bars. Glass shattered. Wood splintered. Walls shook. Men burst through the door and stormed through the ground floor, smashing furniture and hurling it to the floor. Then it was quiet.
Suzanne Jurmain, *The Forbidden Schoolhouse: The True and Dramatic Story of Prudence Crandall and Her Students*

After this attack, Jurmain writes Prudence decided to close the school. Then an ad was placed in the *Liberator*, an antislavery newspaper: "'For sale, the house in Canterbury occupied by … Prudence Crandall.'" The climax in this work of nonfiction is not a happy one.

Conclusions

Strong endings often return to the main themes of a nonfiction work and suggest new beginnings. Sy Montgomery concludes *Quest for the Tree Kangaroo: An Expedition to the Cloud Forest of New Guinea* with advice for kids about becoming scientists and ways they can help preserve wildlife and the environment.

At the end of *Hitler Youth,* Susan Campbell Bartoletti speaks directly to young readers, letting them know that a new beginning is within their power:

Some people wonder: Could another despot like Hitler rise to power on the shoulders of young people?

Only young people today can answer that question. What are you willing to do to prevent such a shadow from falling over you and others?
Susan Campbell Bartoletti, *Hitler Youth: Growing Up in Hitler's Shadow*

Now it's your turn

Last pages and lasting impressions
Make sure your conclusion makes a lasting impression on readers. Be certain you:

- Identify and spotlight its climax
- Suggest any related new beginnings
- Include helpful and interesting additional information such as timelines, epilogues, and perhaps an author's note

After the story is over

Is there additional information or help you want to give readers? Bartoletti includes a separate epilogue at the end of *Hitler Youth: Growing Up in Hitler's Shadow*. It describes what happened after World War II to each of the young people she profiles. Bartoletti also includes a timeline of Hitler's rise to power, the Hitler Youth movement, and the events of World War II.

Sy Montgomery adds a page of information about places to go and Web sites to browse to learn more about tree kangaroos and Papua New Guinea. She has a separate page with information about the language of people who live there. These two authors—like many other writers of nonfiction—also have a concluding author's note that tells a bit about how and why they came to write their books.

MAKE YOUR WORDS WORK

Well-chosen words make non-fiction fun, fascinating, and unforgettable. They stir readers' hearts as well as minds.

A sense of life

Use as many of the five senses as possible to make descriptions come alive. Touch and sound as well as sight help readers experience a summer day long ago:

Saturday, August 3, 1793: The sun came up, as it had every day since the end of May, bright, hot, and unrelenting. The swamps and marshes south of Philadelphia had already lost a great deal of water to the intense heat, while the Delaware and Schuylkill Rivers had receded to reveal long stretches of their muddy, root-choked banks. Dead fish and gooey vegetable matter were exposed and rotted, while swarms of insects droned in the heavy, humid air.
Jim Murphy, *An American Plague: The True and Terrifying Story of the Yellow Fever Epidemic of 1793*

We experience the natural setting that breeds this plague.

Tips and techniques

A metaphor describes something by calling it something else—for instance, a caring person might be called an "angel." A simile describes something by comparing it to something with the word "like" or "as." For example, as hungry as a bear.

Use vivid imagery

Bring scenes to life by creating vivid word pictures with metaphors and similes. Catherine Thimmesh describes the hopes of Team Moon that very soon their spacecraft will land "on that giant glowing ball in the inky-black soup of space." This double metaphor does not mean that the moon is really a huge, lit-up child's toy. Nor does it mean that outer space is really made of liquid food! Thimmesh uses this word picture to communicate how perfectly round the moon appears from a distance—just like a manufactured, bouncing toy.

Similarly, the night sky viewed from Earth seems dense and, if one could only reach out far enough, touchable—just like a thick soup.

Sy Montgomery uses similes to help readers feel and see the unusual shapes of lush forest growth:

Light green fungi feel like the rubbery ears of a grandfather. ... Mushrooms look like little umbrellas, or lace, or the icing piped on a birthday cake.
Sy Montgomery, *Quest for the Tree Kangaroo: An Expedition to the Cloud Forest of New Guinea*

Montgomery uses comparisons with ordinary items—such as ears and umbrellas—to show how extraordinary the Cloud Forest is.

Now it's your turn

Imagine that!

By yourself or with a friend, brainstorm some similes for colors and textures. Make a list of 10 colors and textures. For each word, write down five similes. For instance, "As purple (or yellow or blue) as a ..." or "As smooth (or sharp or rough) as the ..." How could you use these images or ones like them in your nonfiction? Use a dictionary or thesaurus for extra help.

WRITE TO EXCITE

When you write action scenes, excite your readers with your word choice.

Replace everyday action words with bold, unusual ones. Have characters "scramble" instead of "climb" and "scoot" instead of "move."

Susan Campbell Bartoletti uses vivid action words to describe two days of brutal destruction in Germany in November 1938:

> *The rampage continued as the Storm Troopers and SS stormed the synagogue. They smashed the intricate lead-crystal window above the entrance and flung furniture through other windows. Others attacked the Jewish shop owners, punching and clubbing them senseless. They dragged the shop owners, bleeding, to the army trucks and shoved them inside. The Jews were then hauled to concentration camps.*
>
> Susan Campbell Bartoletti,
> *Hitler Youth: Growing Up in Hitler's Shadow*

Bartoletti uses "stormed" and "smashed" instead of the more ordinary "entered" and "broke." She substitutes "dragged," "shoved," and "hauled" for the less vivid "took," "put," and "taken." Her word choice casts this terrible scene in sharp detail.

Now it's your turn

Lively words

By yourself or with a friend, make a list of 10 everyday action words such as *walk* or *run*. Then have fun brainstorming at least four unusual substitutes for each word. Use a dictionary or thesaurus for extra help.

CASE STUDY

Susan Campbell Bartoletti says that "respect for your audience is the foremost requirement for anyone who wants to write." This former eighth-grade teacher says this is also true for teaching. She continues to search for the "untold stories in history" to inspire her books.

Tips and techniques

Warn readers if your books contain words that could offend people. Suzanne Jurmain gives such a warning in The Forbidden Schoolhouse: The True and Dramatic Story of Prudence Crandall and Her Students. She explains that 19th-century Americans used different polite words for African-Americans than people do today. Jurmain also warns that—to be accurate—her book about Prudence Crandall (left) includes the insults that were often hurled at African-Americans.

IN THEIR OWN WORDS
Unlike writers of fiction, nonfiction authors do not make up words and put them into the mouths of their characters.

Tips and techniques
Use *says, said,* or *wrote to introduce quotations. You can sometimes substitute words such as* complained, whispered, *or* shouted *for variety and when they suit the situation.*

All the words that appear in quotation marks in a well-written nonfiction work come from a reliable source, such as letters, diaries, or interviews. The words were actually spoken or written by the person being quoted. Using someone's own words is a great way to give readers a sense of that individual's personality along with information.

High-quality quotations
As a high school senior, wildlife biologist Lisa Dabek helped a scientist studying electric fish. Her "shocking" experiences led to her life's work. Sy Montgomery explains:

> *One really big electric fish lived in a tank in his lab. She [Lisa Dabek] remembers that he told her to put her hand in the tank—to feel how strong the shock was. "I was a little scared, but I did it," she said. "And I felt it! It was a strong shock, but it didn't hurt. And I thought, Wow, this is amazing—and so is this whole world of learning about animals."*
> Sy Montgomery, *Quest for the Tree Kangaroo: An Expedition to the Cloud Forest of New Guinea*

Lisa Dabek's own words here capture her awe and enthusiasm, making this a high-quality quotation.

Use dramatic dialogue

Conversations help readers understand the relationships between people as well as their different personalities. Dialogue also gives readers' eyes a rest as it breaks up the page of narrative (storytelling). Done well, dialogue is a powerful storytelling tool—one that adds color, mood, and suspense even as it moves the plot forward.

Rapid-fire dialogue shows expedition members using teamwork and energy to avoid dangers in the forest:

> But first we'll have to complete the final third of our nine-hour hike—a very steep, difficult walk downhill to the river.
>   Hazards everywhere. "Hole," calls Lisa. "Pass it down!" We've got an early-warning system to alert those behind. "Really slippery rock!" warns Lisa. "Rotten logs!" calls Holly. "Bad mud!" cries Christine.
> Sy Montgomery, *Quest for the Tree Kangaroo: An Expedition to the Cloud Forest of New Guinea*

Follow convention

Dialogue is usually written down according to certain rules. Often a new paragraph begins with each new speaker. You already know that what a person actually said is enclosed in quotation marks, usually followed or preceded by a tag such as "he said" or "she said." Sometimes to give the sense of a real conversation, writers place these tags in the middle of a sentence. This placement adds another rhythm to the conversation, making it more lifelike. Sometimes nonfiction authors use information from their sources to add descriptions of gestures, faces, and actions to a dialogue.

REAL-LIFE WORDS

People's speech often reveals much about their background or current situation. Help readers learn all they can about people in your book through their own, real-life words.

On an expedition in Spanish-speaking South America, an annoyed American explorer and anthropologist, Johan Reinhard (left), speaks in Spanish:

"Diablos!" Dr. Reinhard said. Translation: "Devils!" According to NOVA, he said this each time he encountered an especially stubborn stretch of frozen mountain. Kelly Milner Halls, *Mysteries of the Mummy Kids*

When disaster strikes, a man screams in terror:

Sullivan didn't hesitate for a second. "FIRE! FIRE! FIRE!" he shouted as loudly as he could. Jim Murphy, *The Great Fire*

The people of New Guinea speak a language called Tok Pisin. It is made up of words from many languages, including English. Joshua Nimoniong (right), a guide, speaks:

Joshua, though, has seen many [tree kangaroos]: "Plenti taim mi lukim," he said in Tok Pisin. And then he spoke again through Kuna: "I am happy I saw it today," he said, "and grateful to share it with you. We hope we see more. It's still out there." Sy Montgomery, *Quest for the Tree Kangaroo: An Expedition to the Cloud Forest of New Guinea*

Tips and techniques

Include some words from other languages if these are part of people's speech. Be sure to include a translation, too! Use capital letters or boldface type to indicate shouts.

Rapid chatter

Sometimes authors indicate a fast-paced conversation by removing all tags. Excited scientists chatter quickly when Gabriel Porolak (right) finally locates a tree kangaroo:

> *Then, at 9:07 A.M., the signal swells.*
> *"He's in a tree!" cries Gabriel.*
> *"Yes—but which one?"*
> *"This way—over the ridge."*
> *"Somewhere here, he's hiding."*
> Sy Montgomery, *Quest for the Tree Kangaroo: An Expedition to the Cloud Forest of New Guinea*

By not using tags to identify the last three speakers, Montgomery helps readers feel the excitement in their rapid remarks.

Now it's your turn

"Say that again!"

Try other ways of introducing quotations and dialogue in your book. Use tags in the middle of a sentence or between sentences. Remove all tags to see if such back-and-forth dialogue remains clear and seems more dramatic. See which technique works best at various points in your book.

BEAT WRITER'S BLOCK

Even famous writers sometimes get stuck for words or ideas. This is called writer's block.

If you have been following the writer's golden rule (writing regularly and often), you already have some ways to battle writer's block. Here are some of its causes and other weapons to use.

Your inner critic

Do not listen to that inner voice that might whisper negative ideas about your writing. All writers try out and then throw away some of their efforts. Jim Murphy says that, for him, it takes a "year to do a decent first draft … After this, there are revisions and more revisions. … I'll write a sentence, change it, erase it, and start all over again. And I do this with every sentence and every paragraph I write!"

Also, do not be discouraged if editors turn down your writing. It took several years of effort before Kelly Milner Halls' first work—a magazine article—was accepted for publication. Suzanne Jurmain says, "I collected enough rejection slips to wallpaper my entire bathroom" before an editor finally accepted one of her books.

CASE STUDY

Kelly Milner Halls (right) avoids writer's block through the topics she chooses. She says, "I love nonfiction. And I love WEIRD nonfiction best. I tell people I get paid for being weird and it's not far from the truth. I was a reluctant reader in my youth, so I grew up to write the books I wished I had 40 years ago."

No ideas

Have you run out of ideas? Kathleen Krull says she is inspired by "paying attention—listening, observing—thinking like a writer." Keeping a diary or journal has been useful for her.

As he works on a book, Jim Murphy finds it helpful to consider past suggestions from editors or other people. He remarks, "[A] young reader might write to say she liked or didn't like some particular part of a book, and I'll see a different way to approach material in the future … I try to keep my mind open."

A writer's group

Writing may seem lonely. Some writers take heart by sharing their works-in-progress with other writers. They meet regularly in person or over the Internet with "writing buddies." These critique groups help fight writer's block by sharing ideas, experiences, and even goals. Often, members agree to bring a specific number of new pages to each meeting. Susan Campbell Bartoletti says, "I joined a writer's group and got serious about my writing" before she sold her first work, a short story. Jim Murphy finds it helpful when his wife comments on his manuscripts.

A change of pace

Defeat writer's block by changing your writing habits. If you normally brainstorm sitting still, try walking instead. If you usually like quiet while you write, add music to your personal writing zone. If you write at the computer, try pen and paper. Vary your writing habits for each stage of the process. Sometimes even a very simple change of pace helps. Take a break with a walk outdoors, a jump on the trampoline, a quick video game, or an errand to the store. A short time away from writing may be all you need.

NOW WHAT?

Congratulations! Completing a nonfiction work is a wonderful achievement. You have learned a lot about writing and probably about yourself, too. You are now ready to take the next step in this world filled with fascinating facts!

Another nonfiction work?

Perhaps while researching this project you discovered another topic that excites you. Sy Montgomery (below) says, "One book often leads to another." She considers each of her books to be "a prayer of thanks and praise for this planet and its marvelous creatures of all species." Her most recent book is about her pet pig!

Jim Murphy is "always searching for topics that are inherently dramatic." This author—who has written about blizzards as well as plague and fire—says jokingly about himself, "[M]y friends sometimes call me the Master of Disaster." His future projects include a book about another terrible disease, tuberculosis. You may want to deepen your current interests in nonfiction or explore different directions.

Write related fiction

Perhaps certain events, people, or settings in your nonfiction work caught your imagination. You might want to create your own fiction story about them. Susan Campbell Bartoletti has written a novel inspired by *Hitler Youth: Growing Up in Hitler's Shadow*. Titled *The Boy Who Dared*, this novel is about Helmuth Hubner. This 16-year-old changed his mind about the youth movement and challenged it.

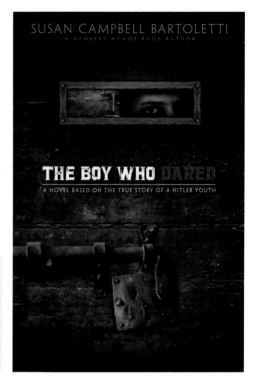

Tips and techniques

Get inspiration and new ideas by examining several nonfiction books related to your topic. For a further lift, try a related work of fiction.

Now it's your turn

Turn fact into fiction!

By yourself or with others, brainstorm your stories with pen and paper. List five events or settings from your non-fiction research on a piece of paper. For the next 10 minutes, let your ideas about people who might have been involved in each event or place flow onto the page. What problems did they face? How could they have solved them? Do not worry about complete sentences or punctuation. You just might find the characters or plot for your novel or short story.

LEARN FROM THE AUTHORS

You can learn a great deal from the advice of successful writers. Almost all will tell you that hard work and occasional failure are part of the writing lifestyle. Yet even though few writers earn enough from their books to make a living, they value their ability to create and communicate through written words.

Jim Murphy

Award-winning author Jim Murphy (below) was not a good student and did not read much until he was 10 years old. That is when his eye problems were discovered and corrected. In seventh grade, a teacher inspired Murphy's love of history. He recalls how this teacher "really started us thinking" when he spoke about how "history books, movies, and … TV" in the 1950s did not tell the whole or true story about Native Americans, other people, and events. Murphy became hooked on reading history! After college, Murphy worked on construction jobs before landing an office job with a book publishing company. He worked his way up to being an editor of children's books. Murphy risked a lot when he left this position to write full-time. He says, "I didn't want to wake up some morning and discover that I was 65 and annoyed at myself because I hadn't taken the chance." Jim Murphy's experience shows that poor grades do not mean lack of ability and that some risk-taking is very worthwhile.

Suzanne Jurmain

As a girl, Suzanne Jurmain dreamed of being a ballerina or an actress. She knew she did not want to be a writer, because she could see what hard work it involved! Jurmain's father wrote—and she saw the way his wastebasket kept filling up as he wrote and rewrote drafts. Yet she loved the stories he told her—some made up and others about "real life heroes, heroines, and villains." Jurmain remembers that "by kindergarten I'd already learned that facts could be as exciting as fiction."

After other careers, Jurmain tried her hand at writing. Her first goal was to write fiction, but it was her nonfiction that publishers bought. Today when asked why she writes nonfiction, Jurmain replies, "I enjoy it. I love to do research. I love to tell stories. And I hope that—like my father—I'll be able to show others that facts can be just as fascinating as fiction."

Gloria Skurzynski

"As much as I admire the work of scientists and engineers and historians and archaeologists, I think my job is the best," says Gloria Skurzynski. "I get to have it all." This author has won awards both for her nonfiction science books and for fiction set in the American West. She uses her enthusiasm for science even in the fiction she writes. She has written science fiction and co-writes mystery novels in which science helps solve the crimes. Skurzynski says she hopes her readers "will be motivated to become creators themselves."

Skurzynski has already directly influenced the career of one successful writer, her daughter Alane Ferguson (right, with Skurzynski). Ferguson has written many books on her own and sometimes collaborates on books with her mother. They advise young authors who collaborate to be great listeners, "respect each other," and "have fun."

Let your book rest in your desk or on a shelf for several weeks. Then when you read it through, you will have fresh eyes to spot any flaws.

Edit your work

Reading your work aloud is one way to make the writing crisper. Now is the time to check spelling and punctuation. When the book is as good as it can be, prepare a final hand-written or computer-printed copy. This is your manuscript.

Think of a title

Great nonfiction titles catch readers' eyes—and sometimes their ears, too! One example is *Tracking Trash: Flotsam, Jetsam, and the Science of Ocean Motion.* The details and rhyme in the title are more appealing than *Floating Ocean Garbage.* It is important to create an intriguing, descriptive title for your book. Think about other titles you know and like.

SCIENTISTS IN THE FIELD

Tracking Trash

Flotsam, Jetsam, and the Science of Ocean Motion

Loree Griffin Burns

Be professional

If you have access to a computer, you can type your manuscript to give it a professional presentation. Manuscripts should always be printed on one side of white paper, with wide margins and double spacing. Pages should be numbered, and new chapters should start on a new page. You should also include your title as a header on the top of each page. At the front, you should have a title page with your name, address, telephone number, and e-mail address on it.

Make your own book

If your school has its own computer lab, why not use it to publish your nonfiction? A computer will let you choose your own font (print style) or justify the text (making margins even). When you have typed and saved the book to a file, you can edit it quickly with the spelling and grammar checker. If it's still not "perfect," you can move sections around using the cut-and-paste tool, which saves a lot of rewriting. A graphics program will let you design and print a cover for the book, too.

Having your nonfiction on a computer file also means you can print a copy whenever you need one or revise the whole book if you want to.

> ### Tips and techniques
> Always make a copy of your book before you give it to others to read. Otherwise, if they lose it, you may have lost all your valuable work.

REACH YOUR AUDIENCE

The next step is to find an audience for your nonfiction book. Family members or classmates may be receptive. Members of a hobby or special-interest group might be intrigued by your work. Or you may want to share your efforts through a Web site, a literary magazine, or a publishing house.

Some places to publish your book

There are several magazines and writing Web sites that accept nonfiction works from young authors. Some give writing advice and run regular competitions. Each site has its own rules about submitting work, so remember to read these carefully. Here are two more ideas:

- Send the opening chapter or concluding chapter to your school newspaper.
- Watch your local newspaper or magazines for writing competitions you could enter.

Finding a publisher

Study the market to find out which publishers publish nonfiction. Addresses of publishers and information about whether they accept submissions can be found in writers handbooks in your local library or on the Web. Remember that manuscripts that haven't been asked for or paid

for by a publisher—called unsolicited manuscripts—are rarely published. When you send a manuscript in the mail, always enclose a short letter explaining what you have sent and a self-addressed, stamped envelope for the manuscript's return.

Writer's tip

Don't lose heart if an editor rejects your book. See this as a chance to make your work better and try again. Remember, having your work published is wonderful, but it is not the only thing. Your ability to write a nonfiction book is an accomplishment that will delight the people you love. Talk about it with your younger brother or sister. Read it to your grandfather. Let your friends read it. Find your audience.

Some final words

Writing a nonfiction work helps you understand more about our world—all the wonderful things people have learned and achieved, plus the mysteries and adventures that still remain. You now have more answers, but you probably have more questions, too! You are better equipped than ever before to find answers to these questions and others that may come up in your life.

Read! Write!

And face life's facts with confidence.

Glossary

chapter synopsis—outline that describes briefly what happens in a chapter

cliff-hanger—nail-biting moment that ends a chapter or scene of a story

dramatic irony—when the reader knows something the characters do not

editing—removing all unnecessary words from a story, correcting errors, and rewriting the text until the story is the best it can be

editor—person at a publishing house who finds new books to publish and advises authors on how to improve their stories by telling them what needs to be added, cut, or rewritten

first-person viewpoint—viewpoint that allows readers to hear someone's inner thoughts or actual speech

foreshadowing—dropping hints of coming events or dangers that are essential to the outcome of the story

genre—category of writing characterized by a particular style, form, or content

manuscript—book or article typed or written by hand

metaphor—figure of speech that paints a word picture; calling a man "a mouse" is a metaphor from which we learn in one word that the man is timid or weak, not that he is actually a mouse

motive—reason a character does something

omniscient viewpoint—viewpoint of an all-seeing narrator who can describe all the characters and tell readers how they are acting and feeling

plot—sequence of events that drives a story forward; the problems that the hero must resolve

point of view—eyes through which a story is told

publisher—person or company that pays for an author's manuscript to be printed as a book and that distributes and sells the book

sequel—story that carries an existing one forward

simile—saying something is like something else; a word picture such as "clouds like frayed lace"

synopsis—short summary that describes what a story is about and introduces the main characters

theme—main idea that the story addresses, such as good versus evil or the importance of truth; a story can have more than one theme

third-person viewpoint—viewpoint that describes the events of the story through a single character's eyes

unsolicited submissions—manuscripts that are sent to publishers without being requested; these submissions usually end up in a "slush pile," where they might stay a long time before being read

writer's block—writer's feeling that he or she can no longer write or has no more ideas

Further information

Visit your local libraries and make friends with the librarians. They can direct you to useful sources of information, including magazines that publish young people's nonfiction. You can learn your craft and read great pieces at the same time.

Librarians will also know whether any published authors are scheduled to speak in your area. Many authors visit schools and offer writing workshops. Ask your teacher to invite a favorite author to speak at your school.

On the Web

For more information on this topic, use FactHound.

1. Go to *www.facthound.com*
2. Choose your grade level.
3. Begin your search.

This book's ID number is 9780756541309 FactHound will find the best sites for you.

Read all the Write Your Own books

Write Your Own Adventure Story
Write Your Own Article
Write Your Own Autobiography
Write Your Own Biography
Write Your Own Fable
Write Your Own Fairy Tale
Write Your Own Fantasy Story
Write Your Own Folktale
Write Your Own Graphic Novel
Write Your Own Historical Fiction Story
Write Your Own Legend
Write Your Own Mystery Story
Write Your Own Myth
Write Your Own Nonfiction
Write Your Own Poetry
Write Your Own Realistic Fiction Story
Write Your Own Science Fiction Story
Write Your Own Tall Tale

Read more nonfiction

Aronson, Marc. *Witch-Hunt: Mysteries of the Salem Witch Trials.* New York: Simon & Schuster, 2005.

Bausum, Ann. *With Courage and Cloth: Winning the Fight for a Woman's Right to Vote.* Washington, D.C.: National Geographic, 2004.

Blumenthal, Karen. *Let Me Play: The Story of Title IX: The Law That Changed the Future of Girls in America.* New York: Atheneum Books for Young Readers, 2005.

Croswell, Ken. *Ten Worlds: Everything That Orbits the Sun.* Honesdale, Pa.: Boyds Mills Press, 2007.

Deem, James M. *Bodies From the Ash: Life and Death in Ancient Pompeii.* Boston: Houghton Mifflin, 2005.

Farrell, Jeanette. *Invisible Allies: Microbes That Shape Our Lives.* New York: Farrar, Straus, and Giroux, 2005.

Freedman, Russell. *Freedom Walkers: The Story of the Montgomery Bus Boycott.* New York: Holiday House, 2006.

Heinrichs, Ann. *The Underground Railroad.* Minneapolis: Compass Point Books, 2001.

Hoose, Phillip. *The Race to Save the Lord God Bird.* New York: Farrar, Straus and Giroux, 2004.

Hopkinson, Deborah. *Up Before Daybreak: Cotton and People in America.* New York: Scholastic Nonfiction, 2006.

Hyman, Teresa L. *Pyramids.* San Diego: KidHaven Press, 2005.

McKinley, Michael. *Ice Time: The Story of Hockey.* Toronto: Tundra Books, 2006.

McKissack, Patricia C., and Frederick L. McKissack. *Days of Jubilee: The End of Slavery in the United States.* New York: Scholastic Press, 2003.

Myers, Walter Dean, and William Miles. *The Harlem Hellfighters: When Pride Met Courage.* New York: HarperCollins, 2006.

Noyes, Deborah. *One Kingdom: Our Lives with Animals.* Boston: Houghton Mifflin, 2006.

Polly, Matthew. *American Shaolin: Flying Kicks, Buddhist Monks, and the Legend of Iron Crotch: An Odyssey in the New China.* New York: Gotham Books, 2007.

Rau, Dana Meachen. *Black Holes.* Minneapolis: Compass Point Books, 2005.

Scott, Elaine. *Poles Apart: Why Penguins and Polar Bears Will Never be Neighbors.* New York: Viking, 2004.

Turner, Pamela S. *Gorilla Doctors: Saving Endangered Great Apes.* Boston: Houghton Mifflin, 2005.

Books cited

Bartoletti, Susan Campbell. *Hitler Youth: Growing Up in Hitler's Shadow.* New York: Scholastic, 2005.

Burns, Loree Griffin. *Tracking Trash: Flotsam, Jetsam, and the Science of Ocean Motion.* Boston: Houghton Mifflin, 2007.

Camper, Cathy. *Bugs Before Time: Prehistoric Insects and Their Relatives.* New York: Simon & Schuster, 2002.

Halls, Kelly Milner. *Mysteries of the Mummy Kids.* Plain City, Ohio: Darby Creek Publishing, 2007.

Jurmain, Suzanne. *The Forbidden Schoolhouse: The True and Dramatic Story of Prudence Crandall and Her Students.* Boston: Houghton Mifflin, 2005.

Krull, Kathleen. *The Night the Martians Landed: Just the Facts (Plus the Rumors) About Invaders from Mars.* New York: HarperCollins, 2003.

Krull, Kathleen. *What Really Happened in Roswell? Just the Facts (Plus the Rumors) About UFOs and Aliens.* New York: HarperCollins, 2003.

Montgomery, Sy. *Quest for the Tree Kangaroo: An Expedition to the Cloud Forest of New Guinea.* Boston: Houghton Mifflin, 2006.

Murphy, Jim. *An American Plague: The True and Terrifying Story of the Yellow Fever Epidemic of 1793.* New York: Clarion, 2003.

Murphy, Jim. *The Great Fire.* New York: Scholastic, 1995.

Owens, Thomas S. *Football Stadiums.* Brookfield, Conn.: The Millbrook Press, 2001.

Skurzynski, Gloria. *On Time: From Seasons to Split Seconds.* Washington, D.C.: National Geographic, 2000.

Swanson, Diane. *Nibbling on Einstein's Brain: The Good, the Bad, & the Bogus in Science.* Toronto: Annick Press, 2001.

Thimmesh, Catherine. *Team Moon: How 400,000 People Landed Apollo 11 on the Moon.* Boston: Houghton Mifflin, 2006.

Walker, Sally M. *Secrets of a Civil War Submarine: Solving the Mysteries of the H.L. Hunley.* Minneapolis: Carolrhoda Books, 2005.

Image credits

Index

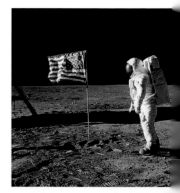